LET'S GO TEAM:
Cheer, Dance, March

LET'S GO TEAM:
Cheer, Dance, March

DANCE Teams

Doris Valliant

Mason Crest Publishers
Philadelphia

Mason Crest Publishers, Inc.
370 Reed Road
Broomall, PA 19008
(866) MCP-BOOK (toll free)
www.masoncrest.com

First printing

1 2 3 4 5 6 7 8 9 10

Library of Congress Cataloging-in-Publication Data

Valliant, Doris.
  Dance teams / Doris Valliant.
      v. cm. — (Let's go team — cheer, dance, march)
Includes index.
Contents: The beginning — Drill teams — Dance teams — Joining a team
— Competitions and camps.
  ISBN 1-59084-540-4
1. Marching drills — Juvenile literature 2. Dance — Juvenile literature.
[1. Marching drills. 2. Dance.] I. Title. II. Series.
  GV1797 .P48 2003
  791.6'4 — dc21
                        2002015960

Produced by
Choptank Syndicate and Chestnut Productions
226 South Washington Street
Easton, Maryland 21601

Project Editors Norman Macht and Mary Hull
Design Lisa Hochstein
Picture Research Mary Hull

Printed and bound in the Hashemite Kingdom of Jordan

OPPOSITE TITLE PAGE

*No matter what style of dance you enjoy, from hip hop to jazz,
modern dance to precision drill, there is a dance team and a
competition out there for you.*

Table of Contents

The Beginning

The dance captain calls out, "Hit!" Step, kick, step-step, step, kick, step-step. Fifty young women stand shoulder to shoulder in a line. With precision and style, they kick in unison, their legs flying high in one fluid movement.

Probably the most distinctive technique used by drill teams everywhere is the high kick. The masters of the high kick are the Kilgore College Rangerettes, who set the standard for dance/drill teams back in 1940 when they first strutted onto the football field at halftime. Their routine brought show business to the football game, and they dazzled spectators with their high kicks.

In order to perform at her best, a dancer needs to stretch often, maintaining and increasing flexibility.

The Rangerettes were the brainchild of Gussie Nell Davis, a graduate of what is today Texas Women's University, who later received a master's degree from the University of Southern California. The Dean of Kilgore College brought Miss Davis to the campus to create a halftime show at football games that would keep the men in their seats.

Miss Davis always believed that dance was the way to entertain sports crowds. Since 1929, she had been practicing this belief as sponsor of the pep club and physical education teacher at Greenville High School in Greenville, Texas. Davis had turned her pep club into a marching pep squad called the Flaming Flashes. Wearing costumes that included caps with a visor and a little feather on the top, they marched with the Greenville High School band.

On September 12, 1940, Miss Davis' first halftime drill team show opened at Kilgore College with 48 members on the line and five officers in the front. They wore red and blue uniforms, white western hats, gauntlets, belts, and boots. Their skirts were scandalously short for the time—barely touching the knees.

That first Rangerettes show wowed the fans with precision military marching, waist-high kicks, and even a fireworks display. Today the Rangerettes have 65 members, with 48 performing each time. Their uniforms have stayed the same, except the skirts have gotten shorter and the kicks have gotten higher.

The Rangerettes have not always performed those head-high kicks. Until the 1960s, high kicks meant waist

The Kilgore College Rangerettes, shown in a photo from the 1950s, at top, and a modern photo, were created by Miss Gussie Nell Davis in 1940 to entertain the crowd during halftime at Kilgore College football games.

high. After Miss Davis saw the Oak Cliff Golden Girls of Dallas, Texas perform kicks way above their heads, she immediately taught her Rangerettes the same kick. They and other drill teams have been kicking that way ever since.

In 1940 Gussie Nell Davis founded the Kilgore College Rangerettes, the first all-girl drill team to perform on a football field. Whenever one of her Rangerettes was ill or could not make a performance, Miss Davis danced in her place.

Halftime at a Kilgore College football game was never the same after that first game, when Broadway-style dance and drill routines moved onto the 50-yard line. Since then, the Kilgore Rangerettes have become one of the most celebrated drill teams in the world, noted for their signature routine, the contagion. With split-second precision, the Rangerettes produce a wave-like motion that fluidly ripples down the line of girls and back again.

About seven years after the Rangerettes danced onto the football field, another precision dance/drill team began impressing football fans. Since 1947, the Tyler Junior College Apache Belles have kicked their heels and rivaled the Rangerettes. Like the Rangerettes, they perform with the school band, never to recorded music. They, too, kick high above their heads and have developed their own trademark styles.

In the 1960s another famous dance/drill team began at Southwest Texas State University (San Marcos), where the Strutters became the first four-year college dance and drill team. Until then, dance and drill teams were found only at two-year colleges like Kilgore and Tyler Junior College.

In the 1990s, the Texas Tech (Lubbock) Gunfire Kickline began performing the traditional high kick and other dance routines. Both the Strutters and Gunfire Kickline wear western-style uniforms and hats, like their junior college predecessors.

Drill teams are such a vital part of the Texas school spirit programs, they have become part of the curriculum. Some junior high and middle schools support drill teams, which are the training grounds for the high school squads. In many high schools, students can receive a required physical education credit for participation on the drill team. If they continue in the program, they can receive a fine arts credit for dance.

Dance teams are an outgrowth of drill teams. They offer a less restricted type of routine. Although dance teams perform synchronized routines, they are less rigid and often lack the military-style kicks and marches. Modern dance and jazz routines have grown in popularity. Many dancers want the flexibility and range of motion and technique that these dance styles offer.

Dance teams are a growing segment of college spirit groups in America and Canada. The DanceUSA.com Web site lists over 280 colleges in the United States and Canada that support dance teams. Many of the Canadian

KICKING HIGH

Before practicing kicks, do some stretching exercises. Stretching and warming up prevent injuries and limber up your body so that you can kick higher. Don't worry if you can't kick more than waist high at first. The more you practice, the higher you'll kick. Try following these high kick techniques suggested by Debbie Byrd of the American Dance/Drill Team School. Soon you'll be kicking high.

- Step forward on the left foot and kick the right leg.
- Step forward on the right foot; step forward on the left.
- Step forward on the right foot and kick the left leg.
- The rhythm is step, kick, step-step, step, kick, step-step.
- As you kick, keep your body straight and tall. Do not bend forward.
- Keep your support leg straight every time you kick. Do not bend supporting knees as you kick.
- Point your toes and keep them pointed from the time they leave the floor.
- Keep the heel of your supporting leg on the floor. Remember—the support heel never leaves the floor.

Wearing their western-style uniforms, the Texas Tech Gunfire Kickline finishes a clogging routine with a smile and a "Gun's Up" motion during halftime at a men's basketball game.

dance teams participate in American collegiate competitions as well.

Whether it's the drill team or the dance team, one thing's for sure. School spirit has more than just the cheerleaders to lead the crowds and raise enthusiasm. Teams marching on the football field or performing a routine on the sidelines at a basketball game definitely pump up support for the home team and entertain the crowd at the same time.

Drill Teams

In 1930, a year after Gussie Nell Davis began directing her Greenville High School Flaming Flashes drill team, another Texan living in a different part of the state had a similar idea. Kay Teer was a 15-year-old high school student who had been elected to a spot on the Edinburg High School cheerleading squad. She was elated to be chosen, but she felt sorry for the other girls who hadn't made the squad. She asked the principal if the school could start a new spirit group to include all those girls who had not been chosen as cheerleaders. The principal liked Teer's idea and agreed to set up this new pep squad. With that decision, the modern drill team began.

Though drill teams are best known for their kick routines, they also use dance styles such as jazz, pom, novelty, prop, military, and lyrical.

A lifelong promoter of drill teams, Dr. Kay Crawford organized a 1,268-member drill team that performed at the opening ceremonies of the 1984 Olympics in Los Angeles. One of her goals was to help make precision dance and drill an Olympic sport.

From her sophomore year at Edinburg High School, Kay Teer Crawford spent her lifetime perfecting drill teams in high schools and colleges. She wrote her master's degree thesis on drill teams, and in 1943 she received a doctorate degree.

For most of her adult life, Crawford lived and worked in Redondo Beach, California. She taught physical education at Santa Monica College. However, she continued to develop the concept of a nonmilitary drill team with girls performing synchronized dance movements. She wrote a drill team curriculum for California high schools and colleges. In 1968, she created Miss Dance Drill Team USA, the first dance/drill competition.

Since that first Edinburg High School spirit group, drill teams have grown to over 15,000 teams nationwide. Many of the nation's drill teams exist in Crawford's home state of Texas, but they are popular in other states, such as California, Iowa, Ohio, Louisiana, Florida, and Nebraska.

Drill teams are usually open to as many as 100 or more young women of all shapes and sizes who are physically fit and have some dance skill. The drill team works with the cheerleaders to build enthusiasm on and off the field. Drill teams participate in parades and pep rallies and they stage pre-game and halftime shows for football and basketball games. In some schools they also support other sports.

Many drill teams attend competitions, and most teams require members to attend summer camps. The drill team director is usually one of the high school teachers, often a physical education and/or dance teacher. The director has several assistants, called officers or managers. Junior and senior drill team members with strong dancing and leadership skills may become officers. Some drill teams are so large they have two groups of officers, the military officers and the social officers. Military officers run the rehearsals and are each responsible for one group, or squad. Social officers assist with motivational activities. A final group of assistants to the director are managers. Managers do not perform, but they handle many of the details to keep the organization running smoothly. Managers help the director and officers. They are responsible for all the equipment, props, costumes, and any other items the team may need to perform. Managers see that all equipment is set up and stored when not in use. They also care for the maintenance and storage of the props and costumes. They travel with the team when the team performs at events away from the school.

Most drill team dance styles come from seven basic categories: jazz, pom, kick, prop, military, lyrical, and novelty/character. Some teams include other forms of dance such as aerobics, modern, tap, folk, ballet, and clogging, an English folk dance performed in special clog shoes.

The early drill teams of the 1930s marched in step and formation with the school band. Their movements were rigid, like a platoon of soldiers marching. Today's routines usually include dance movements. Arms flex and flow as bodies bend to perform the ballet-type motions of lyrical dance. Team members often carry props—short flags, pom pons, or flashcards. Novelty routines follow a theme, using costumes, music, and characterizations. A team might use hats and canes to carry out a salute to Broadway music. As they twirl the canes and flip the hats, the drill team dances together as one moving unit.

Props enhance the theme of a dance. In addition, props can add dramatic effect. For example, in a novelty routine to celebrate Texas, team members move among wooden oil derricks that are spewing out bright ribbons representing oil gushing from wells.

Another way to achieve stunning visual effects is by using pom pons. Some drill teams are solely pom squads, and they always perform with pom pons. Other teams occasionally add poms to their routines. Usually the pom pons are huge vinyl shakers in the school colors. Pom pons emphasize the energetic arm movements of the girls carrying them. They are a colorful, exciting way to get the crowd's attention and rouse school spirit.

The Purdue University Goldusters dancers perform a pom routine while the marching band plays. Like many dance and drill teams, the Goldusters are affiliated with their school's marching band.

Jazz is another popular dance style because jazz often involves exciting props and provides a variety of dance movements. Jazz routines can be quick and sharp, yet dancers still keep movements fluid. Like jazz music, jazz dance is often interpretive. However, jazz routines still require precision, since team members are performing many of the motions at the same time.

The routine most associated with drill team is kick. The Kilgore College Rangerettes, Tyler Junior College Apache Belles, and Southwest Texas State University

The Sam Houston State University Orange Pride Dance Team does some high kicks during its pom routine.

Strutters have perfected a number of kicks that their high school and junior high counterparts also attempt. Kicks can be performed in a connected line with arms placed on the shoulders of the dancers. Drill teams use many different kinds of kicks such as swing, when kicks are performed in a particular direction, or fan, a lift kick where the leg circles 360 degrees. Sometimes kicks are combined with dance steps, but the kick is the focus of the routine.

Ideas for dance routines come from many sources: television, movies, musicals, and other stage productions. Even sports inspire choreographers, the people who design the steps to a dance, to create new patterns. Most drill teams require the officers, director, and line members to attend summer camps and clinics, where ideas abound for new halftime and pre-game programs.

The drill team director should be a professional who has been trained in drill team instruction. The officers chosen by the director must have the dancing skills and leadership abilities to train the line members, the girls who make up the line of dancers in a routine. Many of those line members are first-time drill team members, so it's up to the officer to train her assigned squad.

Rehearsals occur before and after school, up to eight hours a week. Each squad of experienced and new members is led by one of the officers. The captain of the drill team often works with the director to schedule these practices. The captain also makes sure her officers know the routines in advance.

One of the greatest assets of most drill teams is the booster club composed of the parents of drill team members. The booster club helps raise funds, makes costumes and props, sometimes provides extra transportation, and gives much needed time and effort to help the drill team succeed during the sports season. Many moms and dads like being part of the booster club. They find the efforts they put forth are quality time well spent with their children.

Although the drill team is usually female, it may have escorts and managers who are male students. The escorts and managers help move props and set up backdrops and other staging effects so that the performances come off smoothly and effectively. These behind-the-scenes males are essential to helping the drill team perform successfully.

The most famous drill team in the world is the Radio City Music Hall Rockettes, who are known for their precision dancing and high kicks. Their popular Radio City Christmas Spectacular is performed annually at Radio City Music Hall in New York City and other cities across America.

To become a Rockette you must be at least 18 years old, between 5' 6" and 5' 10 1/2" tall, and proficient in tap and jazz. More than 225 women perform as Radio City Rockettes in New York and other cities.

You may never become a Radio City Rockette, but you can become part of your school drill team. The drill team offers an outstanding opportunity to show school spirit even if you don't have the greatest dancing skills or most perfect body.

Drill teams have lots of jobs that young men and women can accomplish. There's no better way to develop

A DAY WITH THE ROCKETTES

At Radio City Music Hall, a Radio City Rockette teaches a Master Class where you can learn original choreography from the Rockettes' repertoire. You go through a mock audition, and have a question and answer session with a Rockette instructor. You also get a Stage Door Tour, a guided behind-the-scenes tour of the famous Radio City Music Hall. Your parents can come along for the tour, but they cannot participate in the Master Class.

Participants must be at least nine years old, but there's no age limit after that, and they must have previous dance training. The Rockette Experience costs about $85, but chaperones can view the class and take part in the Stage Door Tour for about $16.

leadership skills than by becoming a drill team officer or lieutenant. The teamwork skills you learn as part of the drill team and the leadership skills you develop if you become an officer will carry you a long way toward career success throughout your life.

Spirit or Sport?

Dance requires discipline and practice. Dance involves lots of physical activity and creativity, concentration and thought, feeling and emotion. Dances tell stories, set moods, and express emotions through the movements carried out by the dancers. To produce movements that express these feelings and ideas, dancers must make use of their minds as well as their bodies.

Dancing is not always a solo activity; dancers are part of a cast, a troupe, or a team. In many high schools and colleges across the country and in Canada, dance teams have become a way for students to combine movement and emotion while boosting school spirit. Dance teams

Dance teams combine movement and emotion with music, creating a spectacular show for spectators.

25

perform at football and basketball games, and for other sports as well.

Just like playing on a sports team, dance team requires each member to be physically fit. In fact, in many high schools and colleges, dance team, like drill team, fulfills a physical education requirement. In some high schools, it also meets the fine arts graduation requirement. To be fit, a dancer must have strength, flexibility, and endurance. However, dance movements go further than just exercising the body; dance is an art form that is mentally and emotionally challenging.

Dancers develop muscular strength by doing push-ups, leg lifts, and *pliés* (plea-ays), a ballet term meaning the dancer bends at the knees with the feet in different positions. Of course, flexibility is a key component for a dancer who must have a full range of motion. Dancers increase their flexibility by stretching.

Dancers always warm up their bodies with stretching exercises. Then they are ready to twist, turn, bend, and carry out all the different physical motions that a routine demands. If they don't stretch first, they risk serious injury to muscles, backs, and other parts of their bodies.

Dancers need endurance and stamina to accomplish all the vigorous movements that the various dance styles demand. Walking, jogging, swimming, and cycling are ways to increase endurance and build stamina. Dancers must apply the same fitness principles as athletes—the continual push to do more today than they did yesterday.

Technique, the basic physical movements dancers perform, is another vital element for a successful dance

No matter what type of dance you want to pursue, ballet can help you develop discipline and muscle control.

team. Good technique requires muscles that are strong and conditioned. It also involves placing body parts in space, such as moving the arms above the head. Technique is properly aligning the body's torso (the middle part of the body) so that all parts are adjusted and working well together. For example, dancers bend over so that the body is positioned at an angle. Then they transfer their weight smoothly while sliding one hand down to grasp an ankle while keeping the other arm straight above the head. All this is done in one fluid movement that appears effortless.

Making dance movements appear effortless is the dancer's goal. Dancers meet this goal when all the elements of technique come together. Of course, these movements are anything but easy. That's why dancers must practice so much. Members of a dance team must work together, which makes the challenge even greater because many times these movements have to be done all together at the same moment.

To learn technique, break down each movement into smaller parts. Then practice until you can move your midsection, arms, legs, feet, and head with perfect ease.

Many dance teams practice technique by doing technical exercises as part of their warm-ups and center floor work. Eventually, dancers are able to adjust their bodies and place their arms and legs in positions with ease. Practice sessions emphasize correct posture, leaps and turns, and proper alignment, so that the torso, legs, arms, and feet are properly adjusted and in line to work together.

When the body is correctly in line, a dancer produces multiple turns or finds her center of balance quicker. Feet that have been trained and strengthened allow the dancer to jump higher and perform the necessary movements without trouble. A dance team is like a sports team that improves with every practice; the dance team grows stronger and more agile.

Many dance team members also attend dance class in addition to practicing with the team. These classes help improve technique and build muscular strength. Of all the classes a dancer may take, probably ballet is the most worthwhile. Ballet classes teach basic techniques, such as

THE VALUE OF BALLET

Continually practicing basic ballet techniques such as *pliés, relevés,* and *battement* help increase a dancer's ability to vigorously bend and move across the floor. Relevés mean raising the feet and heels to almost an *on pointe* position (standing on the tips of the toes). Relevés help build flexible, strong feet and legs. Pliés, where the dancer bends at the knees, warm the leg muscles and help the dancer line up her body as she practices flexing her knees and keeping her body in a straight, graceful line.

Another basic ballet technique, battement, involves opening and closing one leg while the dancer is supported by the other leg. Performing varieties of battement requires the dancer to work the legs and feet in different movements. She bends her body or knees and stretches her toe to a point, sometimes keeping the supporting leg straight and still, other times bending it at the knee.

Battement strengthens foot muscles as they stretch to hold the different foot positions. Dancers learn to lift and turn out one leg at a 45- or 90- degree angle, pointing the toe, while the supporting leg remains strong and fixed on the floor. In some positions the supporting leg rises, and the dancer raises her foot till she's standing on the ball of her foot. Flexibility, endurance, and strength all combine as the dancer practices these ballet movements over and over.

Building strong legs and feet is very important for members of a dance team. They don't point their toes in ballet slippers; they point in jazz sneakers or other types of dance shoes. Although dance teams don't dance on their tippy toes like ballerinas, they still use many of these ballet movements to achieve the leaps, turns, and fast footwork that are part of dance team routines.

Leaps like this one may look effortless, but they require strong muscles, flexibility, and lots of practice and warm-up.

proper leg and foot motions, correct body alignment, and movement. Practicing ballet positions improves arm movements so that they no longer seem stiff and forced.

Many children start ballet at age three and continue through adolescence into adulthood. Ballet classes help you get an early start if you want to be on a high school dance team. Even if you didn't start when you were very young, it's never too late to join a ballet class and start stretching and flexing those muscles.

Ballet is the basis for much of the dance performed by the dance team. The fundamentals taught in ballet are incorporated in modern and lyrical dance, as well as in jazz movements, hip hop, and other types of dance. Dance team members who have been part of the corps de ballet (the company of dancers) already have experienced teamwork, cooperation, movement to the rhythms and pace of music, and the realization of the dance space around each and every dancer. These are important elements that a dance team follows and uses to execute the variety of dance styles they perform.

Dance teams perform many of the same routines as drill teams, which is why today's teams are often called dance/drill teams. Dance teams do jazz and stylized jazz routines, which may include hip hop and funk. Funk incorporates street dances found in cities across America.

Funk and hip hop may use rap music appropriate to high school or it may create sounds from props that are part of the dance routine, like metal trashcans or other noise-making objects. Dance teams sometimes combine jazz, funk, and hip hop into one routine. Choreographers design movements that match the upbeat, fast-paced energy of contemporary music.

Dance teams kick, too. They use props and may perform novelty routines that thematically interpret music or fit a character. For example, the team might dance to music from television shows and movies about space. The props and costumes that are part of this novelty dance would have a space theme. Dance teams don't rule out even the more military approach that contains sharp arm, head, and leg movements, especially when they are performing a patriotic theme.

Some routines are open, meaning they may combine tap dancing, some kind of production number, or a mix of three or more of the other dance styles. Dance teams are no longer all-girl, either. Some have gone co-ed, with males performing many of the routines with the females.

Modern and lyrical are two dance styles that have become dance team standards. Modern dance uses steps from ballet, but it is not bound by the rules of ballet positions. Modern dance emphasizes letting the body move and fall naturally. Dancers are free to use creative ways to line up body parts and distribute body weight so they can produce distinctive movements. Sometimes modern dancers perform barefoot. Modern dance routines allow dancers to interpret the music and move freely. Routines might include some tumbling or acrobatics.

Lyrical dance combines ballet and jazz techniques. Lyrical dance involves movements that are done in a flowing or continuous pattern as the dancers interpret the music or the words to the music through their dance. Like modern dance, lyrical routines allow dancers to perform original, expressive movements. For example, dance teams might take a popular love song and reveal the emotion expressed in the lyrics through free-flowing arm and body movements that are highly artistic and dramatic.

Costumes and makeup help dancers tell a story, express an emotion, or establish a mood. Costumes are sets in motion since costumes help the audience understand the action and theme of the dance. Costumes should

Hip hop, a style of dance featuring contemporary urban music and upbeat fast-paced steps, inspires choreography and costumes that match the tempo and feel of the music.

never detract from the movements of the dancers; they should enhance the movements so that the audience understands the message.

How the costume fits the body, and the materials used in it, depend on the theme of the dance and the effect the choreographer wants to achieve. Costumes may loosely drape the body, or they may show every curve. Dance teams sometimes perform modern and lyrical dances in all-in-one costumes like unitards because the dancers are

PIONEERS OF MODERN DANCE

Modern dance is a highly individualized form of artistic expression with many different interpretations. Because there are so many ways to describe modern dance, it is hard to pinpoint one particular concept. However, there is one aspect of modern dance that everyone agrees upon—it began as a rejection of the traditional principles of ballet, although modern dancers use many ballet positions in dance movements.

Three women were leaders in creating this new dance form. Isadora Duncan is often called the "Mother of Modern Dance." Duncan was the first to reject ballet rules. She even refused to wear ballet slippers. Instead she danced barefoot. She also refused to wear the tight-fitting ballet costumes. She wore a tunic, a long shirt that came down to her knees. Duncan's ideas shocked many people.

Martha Graham believed that breathing helped create dramatic and powerful dance movements. She called this technique contraction and release. Breathing out is contraction. Breathing in is release. Breathing comes from the torso, or middle section of the body. Graham's choreography used the torso and other parts of the body to create new ways to express movement and ideas.

Katherine Dunham was an alumnus of the prestigious University of Chicago where she received undergraduate and graduate degrees in anthropology (the study of different cultures). Using her dance talents and knowledge of anthropology, she designed some completely new dance techniques based on African and Caribbean ceremonial and folk dances. Combining ballet with African and Caribbean dance traditions, Dunham pioneered a technique that today is an important part of modern dance.

focusing on the body in motion as one moving element. The costume is almost like the dancers' skins.

Funk and hip hop dances sometimes use street clothes as costumes. Dancers might leap and turn in sneakers and t-shirts; or they might perform fast footwork wearing work shirts, baggy pants, and boots.

Whatever costumes dance team members wear, choreographers should choose designs that flatter different body sizes and shapes. Costumes must move with the body and not get in the way of arms and legs.

Choreographers use makeup as a further way to help the audience understand the message in the dance. Makeup can change a dancer's appearance or create a character. Makeup dramatizes the dancers' features. Dance teams sometimes paint designs on their faces that blend with their costumes so that their whole bodies sparkle as they leap, twist, and turn.

Some drill teams have special bright red lipsticks that the team members must always wear when they perform. It helps create the unified look so important in drill team and makes it easy for even the fans sitting high in the stands to see the teams' bright and beautiful smiles.

Some dance and drill teams always wear the same costumes when they perform. The Kilgore Rangerettes are known for their distinctive cowgirl-type costumes which have become a trademark of the Rangerette organization. Many professional cheerleaders wear the same costumes every time they perform.

Dance teams are gaining in popularity everywhere. In Canada, the Canadian College Dance Team Association

Costumes and makeup are important in dance because they help dancers convey a theme. By coordinating eye makeup with their costumes, dance teams give themselves a unified and dramatic look.

is helping to build dance teams. The York University Danz Team is one of its members. This team performs at football, basketball, and volleyball games. They also participate in community and other special events. They travel to the United States to compete in cheer and dance competitions, and they take part in the Canadian Invitational Dance Team Championships. To be a member of this dance team, students must maintain a 2.5 or C grade point average (GPA). When they try out, they must be able to use pom pons and do switch leaps, splits, straddles, and double and triple turns.

In the United States, the Southwest Texas State University Strutters are good examples of what is required to make a college dance team. Strutters must maintain a 2.0 or C grade point average. Dancers must always remember they are performing with a team that works as a precision unit. They must demonstrate dance skills, flexibility, and coordination on an above-average level. Being able to kick high is very important, as well as being physically fit, with strong muscles, knees, and ankles. Strutters must have a positive attitude toward learning and willingly accept constructive criticism. Although there are no height requirements, weight and body shape must be within the normal range for a person's size and bone structure.

High school dance teams echo many of the college requirements. Commitment and practice are number one priorities for dancers who have the technical skills that will enable them to make the team. High school dance teams usually number about 20 individuals. Some large high schools support both drill team and dance team; other high schools often have a dance/drill team that combines the styles of both.

Dance teams offer high school and college students excellent opportunities to grow as individuals, practice discipline, and build teamwork skills.

Joining a Team

You love to dance, and you want to show your school spirit at the same time. You decide to try out for the school dance/drill team.

Although tryout requirements vary, most dance/drill team directors follow similar guidelines. If this is your first year of dance/drill team, you will be trying out for the position of line member. A line member is one of the hundred or so team members who may have to audition each week for a spot in that week's halftime show at the football game. Trying out for the dance/drill team line usually involves dance technique, kick technique, and projection.

Dance or drill team members usually keep their hair neatly pulled back from their faces for competition.

A panel of about four professional dance/drill team instructors, one of whom is the director of your team, will judge your performance. They may expect you to have previous dance or drill team experience, such as a pre-drill class or private dancing instruction at a studio in your community. Judges evaluate your posture, muscle control, body placement, arm and leg movements, toe points, and leg and body extensions. Judges also look for your potential as a dancer and your willingness to take direction from your coach and officers.

Some tryouts use the hat test to judge your kick technique. The hat test means you can kick the rim of your hat with proper kick form. Judges also look for flexibility as you demonstrate your basic kick technique. You may also be asked to do a split.

Judges watch how focused you stay on completing the routine. If you make a mistake in your routine, use this as a positive moment. Show the judges how quickly you can recover and how well you keep your poise. The judges score you on your energy, confidence, winning smile, and elements of audience appeal. Audience appeal will be important as you help your team dazzle all those sports fans during halftime and pre-game shows.

Although your grades are not part of the audition process, dance/drill teams have grade requirements. Most teams specify that members have at least a C grade point average. In some states, this is also the same grade point qualification needed to play on sports teams.

Physical appearance is another concern. Height is not often an issue, but body weight is. Most teams look for

When auditioning new recruits for a dance or drill team, judges and instructors will look for dancers with flexibility.

individuals whose weight is in proportion to their height and body size. Of course, judges will look at the overall picture you present.

Make sure you wear the correct clothes. This is not the time to make a fashion statement. Choose styles that flatter your body shape. Unless you are given specific directions about what colors to wear, dress in basic solid colors like black, navy, or dark gray. Clothes should be clean, neat, wrinkle-free, and without stains or damage.

Developing a fitness routine can help you be the best dancer possible. To make your physical fitness regimen more fun, listen to your favorite music while you work out, or organize exercises that your team can do together.

Don't make tryout day the first time you wear these clothes. Put them on at home and make sure you can stretch, kick, and bend comfortably in them. Plan your wardrobe well ahead of the tryout date so that you know you will look your best. Following these suggestions will help you meet the physical appearance requirement.

Shoes are also important. You may be given specific directions about what shoes to wear. If not, avoid clunky jogging shoes or colorful tennis shoes. Wear shoes that help you gracefully point your toes.

Don't wear any jewelry. Your hair should be neat and pulled away from your face. Swing your head around to make sure your hair will stay in place. Although makeup will be part of the team's dance routine, on tryout day keep your makeup to a minimum. Look natural and let your smile be your best feature. And whatever you do, don't chew gum.

To improve your chances of making the team, attend any clinics and workshops offered by the director and officers. You'll learn the basic requirements and maybe more. Talk to team members. Ask questions about such topics as dance styles, difficult moves, expenses, and grade requirements.

Good posture is a must for a dancer and healthy for anyone. Constantly practice good posture when you stand, sit, kneel, or walk: head up, stomach in, shoulders slightly back but not stiff, rib cage relaxed. Practice looking relaxed and natural.

For hundreds of years women have been told to walk with a book on their head. This advice hasn't changed, so get out a book, preferably a hard-backed one, and walk around, keeping it balanced on top of your head. Watch yourself in the mirror; ask a relative or a friend to judge your posture.

Eat healthy foods. Don't become obsessed about your weight, but keep in mind that most teams want your weight to be in proportion to your height. Remember that healthy foods make fuel for your body. Good eating habits mean strong muscles that give you the power you need to make all those leaps, turns, and kicks.

If you haven't begun a strength and conditioning program, get started—well before spring tryouts. Use your time in pre-drill class to get ready, to create habits that will serve you well and make your body a powerhouse of energy. Jog, walk, or dance to your most upbeat music for about 20 minutes a day. According to Suzanne Doucet, owner of Dance Works and president of the Louisiana branch of Dance/Drill Team Directors of America, "Walking seems to be the all-time best way to keep your body in shape. This, in addition to specialized stretching and conditioning."

Working out is not always fun, but when you finish a good workout, you not only feel better, you also feel better about yourself. According to an article by George Allen on the American Dance/Drill Team Web site, "A workout is 25 percent perspiration and 75 percent determination. Stated another way, it is one part physical exertion and three parts self-discipline."

Even though you will be part of a team, self-discipline is an important part of dance or any activity. You commit to attending rehearsals and practice, often beyond the regular school day. You commit to attending the required sports games and performances, and to helping raise funds for your team.

Dance/drill team participation can be expensive. Costumes, props, music, and other necessities to make each week's performance a success do not come cheaply. Although dance/drill teams have several ways to raise funds, often each team member must agree to pay some expenses. Some teams have membership fees or dues.

Many teams compete, and most require members to attend summer camp, often at the member's expense.

Once you've completed a year on the team and discovered you like it, you may want to try out for officer. Officers assist the director in the management of the dance/drill team. Each officer, often called a lieutenant, is in charge of a squad of girls, and it is that officer's duty to see that her squad has learned the week's routine and completed any other assignments the director gives her. Many schools hold training sessions to prepare officers for tryouts and to make officer candidates clearly aware of their responsibilities.

Officers must know dance terminology and be able to use it. Many times officers select the music and

FUNDRAISING IDEAS

1. Hold a school dance.
2. Raffle off a popular item.
3. Hold a Kick-a-thon.
4. Hold a Walk-a-thon.
5. Sell donuts for breakfast.
6. Sell mums for Homecoming.
7. Sell flowers with messages attached.
8. Create gift baskets to sell.
9. Sell balloons.
10. Offer baby-sitting services at sports events or other places where parents could easily leave their kids and enjoy the event kid-free.

A dance team shows off its poise, style, skill, and smiles at the 2002 National Dance Alliance championship.

choreograph the dances for a show. Officers must know how to select music that will fit the dance styles and theme of a particular show, then chart the melody in eight count intervals or beats of the music. Once the officers have created the routine, they must teach the rhythms and steps to their individual squads.

Many directors interview each officer candidate to evaluate that officer's expertise and leadership potential. In a sense, an officer is like a junior teacher, since she must maintain order and discipline in her squad and teach them the skills and routines they must use on the field.

Officers are chosen by tryout. The director and usually three other knowledgeable dance/drill professionals are the judges. They will be evaluating the candidate's dance technique, kick technique, and showmanship. These are all qualities that each dance/drill team member has displayed in order to be chosen for the team. However, to become an officer, judges also score the candidate on leadership qualities and the ability to perform an original routine that demonstrates the ability to choreograph steps to music.

Once the officers are selected, the judges select the captain. Many teams announce the name of the girl chosen as captain as the final event on the day of officer tryouts. Some teams wait until summer camp to choose a captain. Directors want to see which officer has taken the best leadership role during camp, and that is the officer they name as captain. In whatever manner directors choose their captains, the girl they choose will develop superior leadership skills as she carries out her duties.

Whether you become an officer, or spend three years on the line, you will gain valuable experience not only as a dancer but also as part of a team. In dance/drill, teamwork and precision are important factors. You are not a solo dancer, nor are you trying to outperform the other members of the team. You want to add your skills and showmanship to the other team members so that together you and your team produce a synchronized program that sparkles with excitement and distinction.

Competitions and Camps

5

Whether you are a member of a drill team or dance team or a combination of both, there is a competition and summer camp for you. Performance opportunities exist for all ages from kindergarten through college. Not all teams choose to compete, but for those who do, many organizations provide opportunities to win trophies and ribbons.

Most of the cheerleading associations have dance divisions. For example, the National Dance Alliance (NDA) is part of the National Spirit Group, whose cheerleading branch is the National Cheerleaders Association. The Universal Cheerleaders Association's dance division is

Excited dance team members hold up a trophy they won at the 2002 National Dance Alliance championship.

the Universal Dance Association (UDA). The World Cheerleading Association (WCA) and the United Spirit Association (USA) are among the other cheerleading companies that include dance as part of their spirit programs. Many of these cheerleading companies host national dance championships at the high school and

JUGGLING SCHOOL AND DANCE TEAM

How do dance/drill team members keep up their grades and find time to compete in national championships? The Victoria, Texas Memorial High School Dance and Drill Team, who are six-time national champions, have some good advice.

To win a national championship means many hours of practice. For about eight weeks prior to the competition, the Victoria team spends hours beyond the school day practicing. If any team member's grades fall below the eligibility level (usually a C), that team member cannot dance.

Dancers maintain their grades by taking advantage of any slice of time that opens during a day. For example, those team members who aren't dancing on the floor are sitting in the bleachers or perched on stage, notebooks and textbooks open, concentrating on their assignments and not on what's happening on stage.

Learning to plan, practically living with your student organizer or assignment calendar, is the way to survive. Dance team members become creative in more ways than performing all those beautiful moves on the dance floor. They creatively find time for class, practice, study— and sleep.

college levels. Many also have contests in the youth and "peewee" categories for elementary-age dance teams. AmeriDance, which is part of AmeriCheer, calls its fourth grade and under the "Twinkle" category.

The elementary-age dance teams usually compete in all-star/studio divisions. These all-star dance teams are made up of young dancers from private dance studios or cheerleading gyms with dance programs. These young all-stars usually perform jazz and pom routines.

All-star teams don't stop when these dancers leave elementary and junior high. For example, NDA has all-star divisions through high school for those talented individuals who want to dance but aren't part of a school team. These elite dance teams can go beyond high school. NDA has an open category for high school graduates age 18 and older.

Middle school, junior high, and high school junior varsity teams are usually expected to perform jazz and pom routines. At the varsity level, high school teams must include other dance styles in addition to jazz and pom. Many competitions require varsity high school dance teams to accomplish a routine called Team Performance.

NDA defines Team Performance as routines that clearly use all four styles of dance: jazz, pom, funk, and kick. Team Performance at the varsity level requires a series of kicks and funk routines using the latest street-style progressive movements.

Some organizations focus solely on dance and drill team competitions. Marching Auxiliary Dance (M.A. Dance) sponsors one of the largest national competitions,

Dancers perform at the 2002 National Dance Alliance championship, sponsored by the National Spirit Group. There are separate NDA championships for junior high, high school, and college levels.

the National Dance Championship, held at the University of Texas, San Antonio. Winning teams, officer lines, dance ensembles, and solo performers take home trophies, plaques, medals, and scholarships. M.A. Dance also awards letter jackets to the highest scoring teams in each size division.

Marching Auxiliary Dance also conducts 11 regional championships across the United States that usually involve 35 to 100 teams. The M.A. Dance team divisions are similar to those of the NDA and other spirit companies.

M.A. Dance has added a new division called High School Elite. A high school team can select 10 to 24 of its best dancers to compete against other high schools' top-notch dancers. The dancers on the elite team can compete with their regular team as well.

One of the foremost dance/drill organizations is the American Dance/Drill Team School (ADTS). ADTS offers competitions at the regional and national levels. ADTS Nationals are held at the University of North Texas in Denton. This contest brings junior high, high school, and college dance/drill teams from all over the country to compete. Judges evaluate dance technique, the team's overall presentation, the content (including the dance styles used in the routine), and the precision with which the team carries out these movements.

ADTS holds other competitions for teams beginning at the elementary school level. ADTS will allow dancers as young as kindergarten to compete. Elementary and junior teams are classified by age and usually are all-stars from private dance studios or youth groups.

ADTS high school team divisions are based on team size. The smallest high school team has a minimum of seven performers who can be up to 20 years old. Divisions go up to the Super Large category that includes 50 or more dancers on the team. Performance time for teams, ensembles (duets or groups from three to 20 members), officers, and college teams run three minutes; solo performers have a two-minute limit. Dance routines, which can be co-ed, fall under the categories of jazz, kick, prop, novelty, military, lyrical, pom, modern, hip hop, funk, or open.

The oldest and largest dance/drill team competition in the United States is the Miss Dance Drill Team USA Pageant. Dance/drill teams from all over America gather in Los Angeles, California to compete in the Miss Dance Drill Team USA competition which ends in a spectacular pageant.

In 1967 Kay Teer Crawford, the creator of the high school drill team, conceived the idea for the pageant as part of a college project. Since that time, Miss Dance Drill Team USA has grown from 268 participants to 6,000. That number would grow if the pageant did not limit its entries. To enter the Miss Dance Drill Team USA Pageant, dancers must be 16 to 19 years old with at least a 3.0 (B) grade point average.

High school dance teams compete in 22 categories that include prop and show drill teams, song leaders, cheerleaders, flag twirlers, co-ed, and male drill teams. Miss Dance Drill Team USA has a "Mr." division for all-male dance teams and male soloists. Teams can perform dance movements using military, novelty, high kick, hip hop, and even ballroom dance routines.

Dance/drill team has caught on in other countries as well. Teams from Canada, South Africa, Australia, Mexico, New Zealand, Singapore, Germany, and Lithuania compete in the Miss Dance Drill Team USA International against Miss Dance Drill Team USA winners.

No matter at what level or for which contest a dance team competes, the team hopes to score high, maybe even win an award. In a winning routine, music must be unique and not tunes that have been overused. Music must be professionally recorded, and teams must bring at least two tapes for the competition.

Costume designs should be simple but effective. Before competition day, costumes need to be tried out to make sure they won't fall apart on the dance floor in the middle of the performance. One way to keep the cost of costumes down and the changes quick and efficient is to use a basic unitard (a one-piece leotard that fits the dancer like skin), then accessorize the unitard with different overlays and skirts that change the look for each routine.

If you plan to perform a solo routine in competition, choose music that is refreshing and inspiring. Add variety to your dance movements by remembering to change the pace and level of difficulty. However, don't try to perform difficult moves that you cannot do well. Use thematic music with a unique costume. Dazzle the judges and audience with your personality and facial expressions. This will enhance the dance movements you are accomplishing on the floor.

Pick a costume that flatters your body. The right color for your skin tone is as important as the way the costume hugs or drapes your body. Secure your hair from your face. It doesn't have to be pulled back, but keep it from falling into your eyes.

Work on your leaps, kicks, and turns. Practice pirouettes, dance across the floor, and stretch, stretch, stretch. Once you've completed your stretching exercises, use your warm-ups as a time to practice these techniques. Work on your posture, stamina, and flexibility. Do everything you can to stay focused, healthy, and positive.

Rehearse in a small area (30' x 20') because sometimes the solo preliminaries are held in a small room. The finals usually are danced on a gym floor, so practice your solo routine in both kinds of space. Invite your family and friends, especially those who are your loudest critics, to a preview of your routine. Do this a week or two before the competition so that you can make any needed changes.

Summer camp is the dance/drill team training ground where you learn the different dance styles and create routines for competitions, pre-game, halftime, and spring shows. Most dance/drill teams require their line members and officers to attend summer camp. The number of companies providing dance/drill team camps for college, high school, junior high, and elementary students is enormous.

There are many things to consider in selecting the right camp for you and your team. Which camp will best fit your team's needs and dance styles? Are the instructors highly regarded dance team specialists? How far is the

Dancers perform at a United Spirit Association (USA) event. The USA is one of many companies that sponsor camps for dance team members, offering a variety of clinics, workshops, competitions, and special events.

camp from your home? Can you reach it by car or will you have the expense of air travel?

If a team cannot travel to a camp, many dance companies will bring the camp to it. Of course, private camps are much more expensive, and you will miss one of the best parts of going to summer camp—meeting new people and making new friends.

Whether a team attends a private or a summer camp, they will learn and practice a variety of dance skills that are appropriate to their age and dance experience. Technique is always part of the dance camp program, and skilled dancers will go beyond the basic dance movements to learn specialty routines. Dancers work with different dance styles and get ideas for music from a wide variety of music selections offered at camp.

Camp instructors teach dance teams new routines for basketball games, pep rallies, and football pre-game and halftime shows. Officers get leadership training in many areas to help run the dance/drill team, and advice on how to train their individual squads.

Camps also provide another avenue to national competitions. For example, at National Dance Alliance summer camps, NDA instructors offer talented dance teams bids to the NDA National Dance Championship. Outstanding college dance teams may be invited to the NCA/NDA National Championships in Daytona Beach, Florida. Other dance and cheer companies scout their summer camps for talented individuals and dance teams whom they invite to national competitions and other special events.

Many Canadian college dance teams travel to the United States to attend summer camps. These talented groups receive bids to competitions in the United States. Canada has its own national dance competition, too.

Competitions are wonderful opportunities to learn and grow as an individual and as a team. Attending summer camp is a first step. Competition and summer camp provide dance teams with a way to receive feedback and make improvements. Competition teaches all members how to set goals and work toward achieving them. Even if your team doesn't bring home a trophy, they have won as long as the competition has been a positive learning experience for everyone involved.

In the world of dance and drill team, competition is a way of life. But the competitive experience can be an uplifting one if you focus on doing your very best, win or lose. That way, you'll always be a winner and part of a winning team.

Glossary

align – To put into a straight line.

ballet – A classical style of dance in which conventional poses and steps are combined with light, flowing leaps and turns.

battement – A ballet term for a back and forth movement of an extended or bent leg.

evaluate – To judge something.

execute – To carry out, perform.

fluid – Adjective used to describe something smooth and graceful, such as a dance movement.

funk – A gritty, modern style of music and dance with the feeling and quality of the blues.

gauntlets – Gloves with a long cuff flaring up from the wrist.

hip hop – A style of dance and music featuring contemporary urban music and upbeat fast-paced steps.

interpretive dance – Dance that tells a story.

jazz – A style of dance, usually interpretive, which is performed to jazz music played in a loud rhythmic manner.

kick – A type of drill team routine featuring high kicks and a kickline.

lyrical – A style of dance that combines jazz and ballet techniques as dancers tell a story through their movements.

mentor – A teacher or coach.

military – A dance or drill team style that incorporates sharp arm, hand, and leg movements similar to those used by soldiers on parade.

modern – A natural style of dance that uses steps from ballet but is not bound by the rules of ballet positions.

novelty – A dance routine that follows a theme, using costumes, music, props, and characterizations to express that theme.

plié – A ballet move in which the knees are bent and the body is lowered toward the ground.

pom – A dance routine that uses pom pons.

projection – The ability to demonstrate one's ideas, feelings, and attitude to others, especially an audience.

prop – Any dance routine that utilizes props, such as hats and canes.

relevé – A ballet move in which the dancer's heels are raised off the floor.

repertoire – All the songs, plays, dances, or other pieces a singer, actor, or dancer is ready to perform.

showmanship – Dramatic and effective presentation.

spring show – A performance put on by many dance/drill teams to raise funds and showcase their talents.

troupe – A group of actors, singers, or dancers.

unitard – An all-in-one leotard that covers the legs, arms, and torso.

Internet Resources

http://www.americheer.com

This cheerleading and dance company offers year-round instruction and a variety of competitions, from regional contests to the AmeriDance National Championships.

http://www.danceadts.com

American Dance/Drill Team is a camp and competition company with over forty years of experience offering dance education through summer camps, winter clinics, and a host of dance and drill competitions around the United States.

http://www.dancecheer.net

Dancecheer.net is a virtual dance and spirit community that offers online resources for dance teams, drill teams, color guard, winter guard, mascots, twirlers, and other performance groups.

http://www.mddtusa.com

Miss Dance Drill Team USA is a non-profit organization dedicated to the advancement of students through the pep arts. Founded by Dr. Kay Crawford, the organization holds the Miss Dance Drill Team USA Pageant each year.

http://www.nationalspirit.com

The National Dance Alliance (NDA) is part of the National Spirit Group, a company with over 50 years of experience in the spirit industry. The NDA offers summer camps, competitions, special events, uniforms, and performance and practice wear.

http://www.usacamps.com

The United Spirit Association (USA) holds camps, clinics, workshops, and special events for junior high, high school, and college levels of dance teams, cheerleading, and band auxiliary.

http://www.varsity.com

Varsity.com is presented by Varsity Spirit, a leading supplier of cheering and dancing fashions and uniforms. The Universal Dance Association is part of Varsity Spirit.

Further Reading

Bussell, Darcey. *DK Superguides: Ballet.* New York: DK Publishing, Inc., 2000.

Grau. Andrée. *Dance.* New York: DK Publishing, Inc., 2000.

Peters, Craig. *Techniques of Dance for Cheerleading.* Philadelphia: Mason Crest Publishers, 2003.

Scott, Kieran. *Ultimate Cheerleading.* New York: Scholastic, Inc., 1998.

Tobey, Cheryl. *Modern Dance.* New York: Children's Press, 2001.

Index

PICTURE CREDITS

DORIS VALLIANT teaches English at Easton High School in Easton, Maryland. She writes books for young people and articles for regional publications. She wasn't a cheerleader in high school, but two of her best friends were. She shouted with them at the Friday night football games and performed a skit or two at pep rallies. She loves to watch dance teams perform their exciting routines.